A History of Britain

MEDIEVAL BRITAIN

1066–1500

Richard Dargie

FRANKLIN WATTS

LONDON•SYDNEY

First published in 2008 by Franklin Watts

© 2008 Arcturus Publishing Limited

Franklin Watts
338 Euston Road
London NW1 3BH

Franklin Watts Australia
Level 17/207 Kent Street, Sydney, NSW 2000

Produced by Arcturus Publishing Limited,
26/27 Bickels Yard, 151–153 Bermondsey Street, London SE1 3HA

The right of Richard Dargie to be identified as the author of this work has been asserted by him in accordance with the Copyright, Designs and Patents Act 1988.

Series concept: Alex Woolf
Editor and picture researcher: Patience Coster
Designer: Phipps Design

Picture credits:
Corbis: 4 (Gianni Dagli Orti), 7 (Adam Woolfitt/Robert Harding World Imagery), 9 (David Hunter/Robert Harding World Imagery), 10 and cover (Skyscan), 13 (Michael St Maur Sheil), 14 (Homer Sykes), 18 (Bettmann), 22 (Historical Picture Archive), 25 (Hulton Deutsch Collection), 29 (Fine Art Photographic Library).
Dover: 11.
Getty Images: 8 (Archive Photos), 12 (Kean Collection), 15 (Hulton Archive), 19 (Hulton Archive), 21 (Hulton Archive).
Mary Evans Picture Library: 17 and cover, 20 (Mary Evans/Mary Evans ILN Pictures), 23, 24, 26 and cover, 27.
The Bridgeman Art Library: 5 and cover (Bibliothèque de L'Arsenal, Paris, France, Archives Charmet), 28 (Department of the Environment, London, UK).

Every attempt has been made to clear copyright. Should there be any inadvertent omission, please apply to the publisher for rectification.

A CIP catalogue record for this book is available from the British Library.

Dewey Decimal Classification Number: 941.02

ISBN 978 0 7496 8195 1

Printed in China

Franklin Watts is a division of Hachette Children's Books.

Contents

The Year of Three Kings

The conquest of England in 1066 marked the start of a new age in British history. The Normans brought new laws, a new language and new ideas like feudalism and castles. Wales, Scotland and Ireland were also affected by the coming of the Normans.

Rivals

Crowned at Westminster in early 1066, Harold Godwinson became Harold II and knew he would have to fight that summer to keep his crown. An attack was expected from Viking Norway, where Harold Hardrada or 'stern ruler' believed he had a good claim to the English throne through marriage. Duke William of Normandy also argued that Edward the Confessor (king from 1042–66) had promised him the English Crown in 1051. He even said that Harold Godwinson had accepted his claim in 1064.

A section of the famous Bayeux Tapestry showing the events of 1066. Here the troops of Harold II are seen sailing round the southern coasts, on the lookout for Norman invaders.

'A Season of Battles'

As the Normans were the greater threat, Harold II patrolled the south coast of England with his army throughout the summer months. But the huge Norman fleet was held up in France by storms in the Channel. The Norwegian invasion force appeared first, landing in Yorkshire in September. Marching northwards at speed, Harold II won a convincing but costly victory against Hardrada at Stamford Bridge. The Viking age in England was over, but Harold had lost many fine men. As Harold counted his casualties, news arrived that Duke William had landed over 7,000 men at Pevensey in Sussex. Harold marched his weakened forces almost 400 km (250 miles) southwards to meet the Norman threat.

Senlac Hill

On 14 October 1066, the exhausted English army faced a foe that was greater in number than they were, and fighting fresh. Harold wisely took up a defensive position on Senlac Hill, blocking the road to London. He planned to let the Norman cavalry tire themselves out running uphill against the English shield-wall. After hours of fighting, the Normans pretended to retreat, luring the English foot-soldiers down onto lower, flatter ground. Here they were mown down by the heavily armoured Norman cavalry. Harold was killed, and many of his men slipped away into the forest. The badly damaged body of the last 'King of the English' was identified by his tattoos. Harold's body was buried in his favourite church at Waltham in Essex.

The March on London

Duke William rested at Hastings for several weeks after the battle, preparing his forces for the next phase of the conquest of England. The march on London was delayed by illness in the Norman ranks, probably caused by dysentery, and William himself fell seriously ill. However, the trickle of English landowners offering their loyalty to William grew daily as he approached London. William was crowned King of England at Westminster Abbey on Christmas Day, less than a year after the death of the Confessor.

At the Battle of Hastings, much of the exhausted English army was slaughtered or fled the field in terror.

Timeline 1066

4 January	• Death of Edward the Confessor
5 January	• Coronation of Harold II
early September	• Norwegians land and capture York
25 September	• Harold defeats Hardrada at Stamford Bridge
28 September	• Duke William lands at Pevensey
13 October	• The English army arrives at Senlac Hill
14 October	• Battle of Senlac, later called Battle of Hastings
November	• William moves northwards to London
25 December	• William I 'the Conqueror' crowned at Westminster

Norman Conquest

In a few short weeks, Duke William and his small Norman army conquered all of England. Normans were soon running the government of the kingdom and the Church.

Power Vacuum

There was little resistance to William because the Anglo-Saxons had lost most of their leaders in the battles of Stamford Bridge and Hastings. Some Saxons, such as Wigod of Wallingford, welcomed the Normans. Other Saxon leaders thought that Duke William would be no more permanent than Cnut and his Danes. However, the Normans were kingdom builders and William's army was full of men who expected to be rewarded with gifts of land.

Resistance

Not all Saxons accepted the rule of the Conqueror. In Cornwall the Godwinsons rebelled, and Hereward fought against the Normans in East Anglia. The most serious threat to the Normans was in the north, where the people were mostly freemen of Viking descent. In 1068 and 1069 there were revolts in northern England. William was forced to act. In the winter of 1069, his men brutally attacked the northern counties. Dozens of villages were destroyed and thousands died in this 'harrying of the north'.

A page from the Domesday Book, a land survey of England commissioned by William the Conqueror in 1085. The book gave the English king a clear picture of who owned what throughout the country.

The Abernethy Standoff

The Scots were quick to cash in on the troubles down south. In 1070, the Scottish king, Malcolm III, married into the old English royal family, taking the Anglo-Saxon Margaret as his queen. Their children were given English names to strengthen their claim to the English throne.

In 1072, William met Malcolm at the village of Abernethy near Perth. Malcolm acknowledged William's supremacy over his southern lands in Lothian. William noted that the Scots and their Flemish allies were a prickly foe and decided to strengthen his northern border with new castles.

Normanization

In the first years of William's reign, leading Englishmen kept their lands. After 1070 however, William stripped many Saxon lords of their estates. Within a few years the old Anglo-Saxon thanes (landowners) were replaced by Norman lords. In the Church, Lanfranc of Caen became Archbishop of Canterbury and supported new monasteries with links to France. Latin and Norman French replaced Anglo-Saxon as the languages of government and the Church.

Norman Castles

The Normans were warrior people of Viking origin. Norman kings granted land to their lords. In return, the lords provided the kings with armed knights. To hold on to their lands, Norman lords built castles, first from earthen mounds and stockades, then later with stone keeps. These castles were not just for defence – they were control centres. From his castle base, the local lord would ensure that the wealth from the castle's lands was used to feed and equip fighting men and horses for war. After 1086, the *Domesday Book* gave the Norman kings in London information about the wealth of every farm in England.

The Norman legacy of castles and keeps, such as this one at Chepstow in Wales, endures to this day.

The Kingdom Builders

In the early 12th century, two intelligent kings ruled England and Scotland, and laid down sound foundations for their successors.

'Beauclerc'

The fourth son of the Conqueror, Henry was well educated because he was expected to become a priest. He was nicknamed 'Beauclerc' or well learned. When William II died in a hunting accident in 1100, the English Crown should have passed to Henry's older brother, Robert, but he was away on crusade. Knowing that many of the English nobles favoured Robert, Henry won their support by granting them new rights and privileges. At his coronation, Henry accepted that there were limits to the king's powers over the nobles and the Church.

Henry I ('Beauclerc') was the first Norman king to be born in England. He strengthened his position as sovereign by marrying Edith of Scotland.

The Exchequer

Henry depended a lot on his ministers such as Roger, Bishop of Salisbury, originally a Norman parish priest who had impressed the king with his energy and enthusiasm. Roger held the important post of chancellor. Twice a year, every royal official had to show him that they had spent the king's money wisely. These meetings were held across a long, wooden table covered in checked cloth, from which the term 'the Exchequer' derives.

Saxon and Norman

Henry was the first Norman king born in England and the first to speak English. During his long reign, the differences between the English and the Normans slowly began to fade. He married a Saxon princess, Edith of Scotland, to merge the old and new royal families of England. Often away visiting his lands in France, Henry appointed a trusted official called the justiciar to make sure that England was governed well in his absence. Henry also took an interest in the local government of his kingdom, sending his officials to judge disputes and curb the power and influence of local lords.

Carlisle Castle, where King David I of Scotland died in 1153.

David the Great

Like Henry, David I of Scotland was a well educated younger son who came to the throne after the early deaths of his brothers. David copied many Norman ways of governing. He granted trading privileges to the largest burghs in his kingdom, minted silver coins and encouraged fairs to attract English and European merchants to his realm. He used Norman and Flemish soldiers to police the rebellious Gaels and Galwegians on the lawless edges of his kingdom. In 1130 he brutally put down the revolt of the independent Moraymen and gave the county to castle-building knights like Freskin de Moravia. David was very generous to the Scottish Church, helping it to build new abbeys. While his friend Henry 'Beauclerc' lived, the border between Scotland and England was at peace. David only set about extending his realm southwards after Henry's death in 1135. David died in 1153 at Carlisle Castle, his favourite and most southern possession.

Timeline

1100	• Henry I crowned at Westminster three days after death of William II
1100	• Henry marries the Saxon princess, Edith of Scotland
1124	• David I becomes King of Scots
1130	• The date of the oldest surviving Exchequer records, the 'Pipe Rolls'
1139	• David acquires the county of Northumbria for Scotland
1153	• David dies and is buried at Dunfermline Abbey

England and France

For much of the Middle Ages, the kings of England owned large parts of France. Over time, however, the richest territories slipped from English hands.

The French Prince

Henry II became King of England in 1154 and Lord of Ireland in 1171. But as he was born and raised in France, he was very much a French prince. He owned Normandy and the rich province of Anjou. His wife Eleanor owned Aquitaine, Touraine, Gascony, Maine and Poitou. Not surprisingly, Henry spent only thirteen years of his thirty-five-year reign in England.

The Loss of Normandy

Henry's sons failed to keep these lands together. Richard the Lionheart spent years away on crusade. In his absence, the King of France took back much of Richard's land. Richard's brother, John, also met with disaster. In 1204, French troops captured the fortress of Chateau Gaillard that protected Normandy. Soon afterwards Anjou, Normandy and much else were lost. John's hopes of winning back these lands ended in defeat at Bouvines in 1214. Expensive expeditions to France by Henry III in the 1230s and 1240s simply emptied the royal treasury and bred resentment in England.

Looking towards France: the castle keep at Dover was built during Henry II's reign. Dover Castle occupies a strategically vital site on the English coast, at the point of departure for the shortest sea crossing between England and the continent.

The Hundred Years' War

In 1337, Edward III went to war to win back the lost lands in France. The war began well for Edward. His Welsh longbowmen (archers using large, powerful, hand-drawn bows) destroyed the French cavalry at Crécy in 1346 and at Poitiers ten years later. By 1360 Edward had recovered much of the old French 'empire'. However, the wheel of fortune turned against him. After a lifetime of campaigning, Edward was forced to ask for peace in 1375. The only French lands that remained in his control were the ports of Bordeaux, Calais and Bayonne.

Agincourt

In 1415 the young warrior king, Henry V, tried to win back the French lands that had belonged to his ancestors. At Agincourt near Calais, Welsh longbowmen again won the day for an English king. By 1419, Henry had retaken much of Normandy. In 1420 he was about to unite France and England by marrying the daughter of the French king when he fell ill with dysentery and died. By 1453, Henry's gains in France, apart from Calais and the Channel Isles, had been lost forever.

The Price of War

Wars overseas were expensive and King John's failures in France led many English nobles to rebel against him. In 1215 they forced him to accept limits to his power. These limits were set down in Magna Carta (see pages 28-9). Henry III was strongly criticized for raising taxes to pay for war in France. Even the House of Commons in Parliament complained about the high cost of royal wars in 1376.

Richard I, known as 'the Lionheart', is famous for his adventures on crusade. A true medieval warrior king, he led his knights in battle in the Holy Land.

Timeline

1154	• Henry II adds England to his continental possessions
1204	• King John loses control of Normandy and Anjou
1259	• English possessions in France reduced to Gascony and Aquitaine
1360	• Treaty of Bretigny marks English high point in the Hundred Years' War
1415-20	• Henry V recaptures lands in Normandy after Agincourt
1453	• English lands in France lost during the minority (childhood reign) of Henry VI

Medieval Ireland

In the 12th and 13th centuries, English kings tried to make Ireland into a Norman-style kingdom. Over time however, these efforts failed and the Irish strengthened their grip on their homeland.

The Tuaths

In 1100, Ireland was divided into more than eighty tuaths, or petty kingdoms and lordships. The rulers of these lands were often of mixed Norse and Irish blood. According to ancient Gaelic custom, the freemen of the tuaths elected their kings. However, in the 1160s English kings began to enforce their claim to rule Ireland.

Strongbow

In 1166 Diarmit, King of Leinster, asked the English king, Henry II, for help against his enemies. Three years later, an army of 600 Anglo-Norman knights under Richard de Clare landed near Wexford to help Diarmit's – and Henry's – cause. The force included many archers (which is how de Clare earned the nickname of Strongbow). By 1171, Diarmit and de Clare had captured Wexford, Waterford and the main town of Dublin.

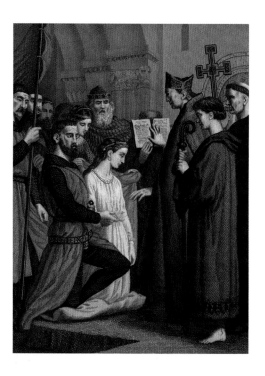

Aoife, daughter of Diarmit, the Irish king, weds Richard de Clare ('Strongbow') in 1170. This marriage forged a strong alliance between the two lords.

Lord of Ireland

When Henry II landed at Waterford he became the first English king to step onto Irish soil. He received the homage of many of the petty kings of eastern Ireland and granted the lands of Leinster to de Clare. However, the title of Lord of Ireland was given to Henry's younger son John, later King of England. John twice visited his Irish lands to build forts and castles there.

Anglo-Norman Ireland

The Anglo-Norman conquest of Ireland was rapid for several reasons. The local Irish nobles were divided and lacked the skills in warfare of the English incomers, who built strong castles such as Carrickfergus. New roads and bridges made trade easier. Silver coins were introduced in the 1180s and royal officials in Dublin upheld the law. By the 1280s, much of Ireland was held by nobles who supported Anglo-Norman control. Native Irish lands were limited to the south-west and the lands of the Ui Neill in the north.

The Bruce Invasion

After 1280, there was an increase in Irish resistance to the Anglo-Norman invaders. From 1315 to 1318, Edward Bruce, brother of King Robert, also led a powerful Scottish army against the English in Ireland. Many Irish lords sided with the Scots, and the three-year campaign did much to loosen the Anglo-Norman grip on Ireland.

Beyond the Pale

After 1330, the English struggled to keep their hold on Ireland. The plague, or Black Death, swept through the cramped towns and claimed the lives of many English settlers there. By 1400, several royal fortresses had been lost. Many Anglo-Irish lords gradually adopted the Irish language and customs. English control was limited to the Pale, the fortified lands around Dublin. Beyond the Pale, Gaelic lords ruled most of Ireland with little interference from the royal officials in Dublin.

Built in 1177, Carrickfergus Castle was an important Anglo-Norman stronghold in Ireland.

Timeline

1166	• Diarmit of Leinster appeals for English support
1169	• Arrival of Richard de Clare's forces at Bannow Bay
1170	• De Clare captures the old 'Norse' kingdom of Dublin
1171	• Henry II lands at Waterford
1180-1280	• Normanization of the eastern counties
1180s	• Introduction of silver coinage
1315-18	• Campaign of the Scots in Ireland
1350-1400	• Rise of Gaelic and Anglo-Irish lords

Medieval Wales

After two centuries of struggle, the Welsh lost their independence in the 1280s, but their language and sense of nationhood were preserved.

This carving of saints from a Welsh holy shrine shows how important religion was to the people of medieval Wales.

Marcher Lords

William the Conqueror made no attempt to invade Wales and was happy to work with friendly Welsh princes, like Rhys ap Tewdwr. Nevertheless, William and his successors set up marcher, or border, lordships. A strong marcher lord like Roger, Earl of Shrewsbury, had almost the same rights and powers as the English king. He could build castles, found towns and wage war without royal permission. Marcher lords also encouraged English and Flemish settlers to live in new towns protected by *mottes* (fortifications).

The Welsh Church

Welsh priests had always been in charge of their own local churches. However, after 1100 the Welsh Church came under the control of bishops who obeyed the English Archbishop of Canterbury. There were also new orders of monks from Europe, like the Cistercians who were as famous for their farming and business skills as for their devotion to God. Norman and Welsh lords invited these energetic and practical men to found abbeys such as Neath, Margam and Strata Florida near Tregaron.

Lleywelyn the Last

Powerful kings such as Henry I captured important Welsh towns such as Carmarthen and forced the people to obey them. But Welsh princes were quick to

Timeline

1070	• Roger the Great becomes marcher Earl of Shrewsbury
1081	• Rhys ap Tewdwr, Prince of Deheubarth, meets with William I
1109	• Henry I extends English influence deep into Wales
1129	• Cistercian abbey founded at Neath in Glamorgan
1260	• Llywelyn recognized as Prince of Wales
1282	• Death of Llywelyn, the last independent Welsh prince
1280s	• Edward I conquers northern Wales
1350	• Likely death of Dafydd ap Gwilym in the great plague

spot moments of English weakness. Numerous strongholds were taken back when the English were busy with a civil war in the 1140s. Llywelyn the Great destroyed many English forts and settlements and retook the lands of Gwent in the 1230s. Llywelyn ap Gruffydd 'the Last' also won back much of the territory lost to the English marcher lords and even got the English to grant him the honoured title of Prince of Wales in the Treaty of Montgomery.

A Conquered People

This high point in Welsh fortunes was short-lived. In the 1270s and 1280s, the English invaded Gwynedd, the heartland of Welsh resistance, and built a great chain of stone castles to defend their conquest. The Welsh retreated to their last refuge – the mountainous wilds of Snowdonia. The English could now put down Welsh revolts more easily and they imposed their law and ways of government on the Welsh. Nevertheless, the Welsh identity was secure for they shared a language and a sense of nationhood that bound them together.

The Cultural Flowering

Although the Welsh lost their independence in the 1280s, the following decades saw a flowering of Welsh literature that reached its peak in the work of Dafydd ap Gwilym (1315-50), one of the great poets of medieval Europe. As in Ireland, Anglo-Norman lords gradually appreciated and absorbed the rich local culture.

The head of Llywelyn the Last is paraded through the streets of London after his defeat and death in 1282.

Medieval Scotland

The kingdom of Scotland adopted Norman ways and prospered as a result. In the Highlands, the Gaelic and Norse peoples created a different way of life.

Normanized Scotland

A French visitor to Scotland in 1250 would have felt much at home. Knightly families with French names held the better land and lived in castles. Royal sheriffs enforced the law. Trade was regulated by royal charter and made easy by silver coinage. The king and his nobles used the languages of French and Latin. Cistercian monks from Europe were busy spreading their religious beliefs and farming Scottish land. Scotland had adopted many new Norman ideas.

Trading Success

This Normanization made the Scottish kingdom successful. Ports such as Berwick and Aberdeen enjoyed a thriving export trade with Europe in timber, fish, leather and wool. Coals from Fife and the Lothians were sent to London. In the 1370s, over two million fleeces were exported each year. Companies of German and Flemish wool merchants lived in their own 'national' halls within the walled seaport of Berwick, which paid over £2,000 each year in customs duties to the Scottish treasury. By 1400, Scots merchants were a common sight in the cities of northern Europe and the market towns of France.

Jedburgh Abbey was one of many magnificent buildings in medieval Scotland that were influenced by French and English styles of architecture.

Gaelic Scotland

Another Scotland existed above the Highland line, far from the Normanized burghs of eastern Scotland. Gaelic and Norn were spoken here, not Inglis (a northern version of English) and Scots. The Celtic and Norse elements in the Highland population had merged to produce a rich Gaelic civilization that loved music, poetry, storytelling and learning. The arts of war were also valued. Power here lay in the hands of great chiefs such as Somerled, who led his impressive force of Gaelic, Norse and Irish warriors deep into the Clyde valley in 1154.

The Highland Chieftains

Long wars between Scotland and England from 1296 to 1357 gave the Highland chieftains an opportunity to build up their power. Chiefs such as the MacDonalds, who backed the victorious House of Bruce, were rewarded with lands and influence. By 1400, the MacDonalds controlled almost all of western Scotland. Thanks to their fleet of swift *birlinns*, the MacDonalds were almost as powerful as the King of Scots. A MacDonald army that planned to attack the rich burgh of Aberdeen was only stopped with great difficulty at the bloody Battle of Harlaw in 1411.

The End of Norse Scotland

Until the 1260s, much of western Scotland still owed allegiance to the King of Norway. In 1266, Norway sold the Hebrides to Scotland for 4,000 merks (an ancient coinage). The bankrupt Christian of Denmark sold off the rights to the Orkney and Shetland Islands in 1468–9. This marked the end of the Scandinavian age in Scotland.

William I of Scotland, known as William the Lion, struggled throughout his long reign to curb the power of the northern chieftains.

Timeline

1154	• Lowland Scotland invaded by Somerled's Gaelic army
1170s	• William I of Scotland campaigns in the northern Highland counties
1266	• Magnus VI surrenders the Hebrides and Isle of Man to Scotland
1295-1356	• Scotland invaded by Edwards I, II and III
1249-86	• 'Golden Age' under Alexander III
1411	• Battle of Harlaw saves Aberdeen from attack by Highlanders
1468-9	• Scottish Crown acquires Orkney and Shetland from Denmark

The Plantagenet Dream of Empire

In the late 13th century, Edward I tried to create a unified kingdom throughout Britain. The warlike Plantagenet king furiously attacked Scotland and Wales.

The Crushing of the Welsh

In 1277, Edward's army marched into Gwynedd, the mountainous heart of northern Wales. After defeating the Welsh princes he forced them to pay homage to him in public. When they rose up against him in 1282, they were savagely tortured and executed as traitors. Edward's military architect, Master James of St George, was ordered to build a chain of stone castles across North Wales. To show that he was now master of the Welsh, Edward gave the title of Prince of Wales to his English son in 1301.

Robert the Bruce encourages his troops before the Battle of Bannockburn in 1314.

Overlord of Scotland

In 1286, Alexander III of Scotland died when his horse stumbled over a cliff. Edward planned to unite the two kingdoms by marrying his son to Margaret, heiress to the Scottish throne, but she died in Orkney the following year. This left thirteen nobles with a claim to the Scottish Crown. Edward was invited to select the noble with the best claim. He used this opportunity to force the Scots to recognize him as overlord of Scotland, then selected John Balliol as king. Edward expected Balliol to be a puppet king who would help him attack France. He was outraged when Balliol negotiated independently with the French king in 1295.

Domination of the Scots

Edward's response was ruthless. He ordered an attack on the rich trading port of Berwick and the massacre of all its inhabitants, an event that horrified Europe. Over 1,500 leading Scots were forced to put their seal to an oath of loyalty to Edward. The Great Seal of Scotland, the symbol of Scotland's independence, was shattered. The records and charters of Scotland were removed to London, as were the Scottish regalia used in the ceremonies to crown the King of Scots. In Edward's letters, Scotland was referred to as a mere lordship, rather than as a kingdom. Publicly humiliated and forced to abdicate, Balliol was to be the last King of Scots. An English governor would rule Scotland instead.

Freedom at Bannockburn

Edward's ruthlessness sparked a national revolt led by Andrew, Earl of Moray, and William Wallace, a lowland landowner. With Edward in Flanders, they defeated an English army at Stirling Bridge in 1297. Edward defeated the Scots the following summer, however, and when he was captured in 1305 Wallace was horribly tortured and mutilated before being executed. Now Robert the Bruce, an experienced warrior, picked up the banners of Scotland. A successful guerrilla campaign gave Robert control of almost every castle in Scotland and he won a crushing victory over Edward II at Bannockburn in 1314.

Timeline

1277	• Princes of Gwynedd defeated by Edward I
1282	• Execution of David, last of the Welsh rebels
1283	• Harlech, Conwy and Caernarfon castles begun by Edward
1292	• Edward selects John Balliol as King of Scots
1296	• Berwick sacked by Edward's army
1297	• William Wallace defeats English at Stirling Bridge
1301	• Title of Prince of Wales bestowed upon the Plantagenet prince
1305	• Wallace betrayed and murdered in London
1307	• Death of Edward I at Burgh-on-Sands in Cumbria
1314	• Scottish independence secured by victory at Bannockburn

At his trial in London, William Wallace boldly rejected the charge of treason, claiming he had never sworn allegiance to the English King Edward I.

The Black Death

In 1348, the bubonic plague – or 'Black Death' – arrived in England. It brought about terrible suffering and loss of life, and had far-reaching effects on the social and political order of Britain.

'Pestilence'

The plague arrived in England at Melcombe in Dorset, probably carried on a merchant ship from Gascony. From there it spread to Bristol, where 'the living were scarce able to bury the dead and grass grew in the High St'. So many priests fell ill that there were too few to bury the dead and the local bishop allowed all Christians, even women, to hear the confessions of the dying.

'Our Great Grief of 1349'

By July 1349 the sickness had spread to Oxford, where the local chronicler recorded that 'the school doors were shut'. At Winchester, the population fell from 8,000 to 2,000. The narrow lanes and cesspools of London were a welcoming environment for the rats and fleas that carried the disease. New cemeteries at Smithfield and Spittle Croft were soon overflowing. Over 30,000 of London's population of 70,000 perished. The rich fled the towns for sanctuary in the countryside, but there was little safety there either. In the village of Crawley, Hampshire, the population fell from 400 to 150.

A father carries his plague stricken child through the streets of London in 1349. The man in the background covers his face in an attempt to avoid catching the disease. The door next to him has a cross painted on it, to show that the house has plague victims inside.

Crossing the Border

In summer 1349, a Scots army gathered at Selkirk near the border, planning to add to English woes. The Scots promptly caught 'the foul deth of the Yngles' and the terror stricken troops spread the disease throughout Scotland. Nevertheless, Scottish chroniclers recorded lower levels of plague death in Scotland than elsewhere. The disease travelled less easily through a land of scattered villages where large settlements were few and far apart. In Ireland, too, the Anglo-Irish who lived in towns were badly affected, yet the native Irish in the countryside suffered much less.

Life After the Death

Towards the end of 1350, the 'great mortality' faded, but it returned in 1361 and again in the 1370s. The plagues hit the urban poor hardest, although those few workmen who survived could demand higher wages. Parliament tried and failed to limit labourers' wages by passing laws. Many merchants also made a lot of money by charging higher prices for their goods.

'The Rootless Phantom'

The Welsh poet Jeuan Gethin, who himself died suddenly in 1349, left a chilling record of the fear that swept across Britain in the year of the plague: 'We see death coming into our midst like black smoke, a plague which cuts off the young, a rootless phantom which has no mercy for fair countenance. Woe is me of the shilling in the armpit . . . the burden carried under the arms . . . a white lump . . . a small boil that spares no one . . . a burning cinder . . . an ugly eruption that comes with unseemly haste.'

In spite of prayers of deliverance offered up by members of the Church, huge numbers of people died from the plague.

Kings and Nobles at War

The kings of England and Scotland often had trouble from unruly barons. However, the War of the Roses was a major crisis that disturbed the peace of England for decades.

The Root Cause

France, Spain and Scotland all suffered from power battles among nobles in the 15th century. However, the struggle between the Houses of York and Lancaster lasted more than three decades and seriously weakened the government of England. The war stemmed from the downfall and murder of Richard II in 1399. His successors, Henry IV and Henry V, were strong kings and few questioned their right to rule. Civil war broke out only during the disastrous reign of the incompetent Henry VI.

This engraving illustrates the story of Richard II's murder at Pontefract Castle in Yorkshire.

Fortunes of War

In the first phase of the war, Richard of York pressed his claim to the throne, but was defeated at Wakefield in 1460. Richard's son avenged his father at Towton the following year. With the support of the 'kingmaker', Richard Neville, Earl of Warwick, he ruled for the next nine years as Edward IV. When Warwick switched to the Lancastrian cause in 1470, Edward was deposed and exiled to Burgundy. Henry VI was briefly restored until Edward returned the next spring and defeated Warwick at Barnet. Henry's wife, Margaret, fared no better at Tewkesbury in 1471. Henry was finally murdered in the Tower of London and Edward ruled until his early death in 1483. His brother, Richard III, was a brave and experienced soldier but he was betrayed and defeated at the hands of Henry Tudor at Bosworth in 1485.

The Cost of Civil War

England was badly damaged by these years of conflict. The battles involved larger armies than any seen on British soil before. The war was especially brutal and people at the time were shocked by the bloodshed. As the war lurched from one phase to the next, there was no shortage of English exiles at the courts of France and Burgundy, looking for troops and support. Foreign mercenary armies ravaged the English countryside.

The Douglas Threat

In Scotland, the Stewart kings had aristocratic difficulties of their own. The powerful House of Douglas had important family members in every part of the realm, as well as massive strongholds such as Tantallon in Lothian. In 1400, the most powerful man in Scotland was not the king, but Archibald the Grim, the Douglas earl who could insult the Stewart kings from his 'island' fortress of Threave. To counter this threat, the Stewarts had to invest heavily in troops and artillery and raise a new breed of dependable nobles such as the Earls of Campbell. Nevertheless, James III was defeated and murdered at Sauchieburn in 1488 by an army led by rebellious nobles.

King Richard III of the House of York was killed at the Battle of Bosworth in 1485. Here he is about to be despatched by Lancastrian soldiers.

Rulers of England 1399-1485

Lancaster	**Henry IV (1399-1413)**
Lancaster	**Henry V (1413-22)**
Lancaster	**Henry VI (1422-53 - falls ill)**
York	**Protector Richard, Duke of York (1453-55)**
Lancaster	**Henry VI (restored to power in 1455, deposed in 1461)**
York	**Edward IV (1461-70 - deposed)**
Lancaster	**Henry VI (restored to power in 1470, murdered in 1471)**
York	**Edward IV (regains power 1471-83)**
York	**Edward V (April-June 1483 - disappears)**
York	**Richard III (1483-85 - dies in battle)**

Population and Economy

The Middle Ages saw a great rise in the number of people living in Britain and changes in the way they made a living. In the countryside, farming methods were modernized; in towns and cities, trade was brisk.

How Many People?

We do not know how many people lived in medieval Britain. Some historians think there were about four million in England in 1290. Scotland probably had a million inhabitants at the time of the English invasion in 1296, and there were about 400,000 people living in Wales in the 1280s. England was the most populous part of medieval Britain. Meanwhile, over twenty million people were living in medieval France.

The Growing Towns

With more than 70,000 inhabitants in 1300, London was unrivalled among British towns. The next largest 'English' town was Bordeaux in Gascony, which had a population of 30,000. Scottish towns were even smaller, for most Scots lived in the countryside. The largest

Towns were growing in the Middle Ages. Nevertheless, the vast majority of the population worked the land in the countryside.

burghs in Scotland – Berwick, Aberdeen and fast-rising Edinburgh – each had fewer than 5,000 inhabitants. After 1250, pilgrimage centres such as Lincoln, Canterbury and St Andrews grew steadily in size, but busy market towns grew faster. By 1290 there were more than 600 English chartered boroughs and over 2,400 settlements holding markets. Despite this, only 10 per cent of the population lived in towns. Most of our medieval ancestors were peasants.

Wool and Trade

The wool trade with Europe was the richest business in medieval Britain. Eastern ports, such as the wool town of Boston, traded with the textile markets in the Low Countries, while the Scots increasingly traded in Denmark and the Baltic area. Ships from English ports also carried wine from Gascony and Portugal.

Village Life

In the years between 1100 and 1400, new ways of farming had a big impact on food production. The rising population created good prices for farm products, and the area of farmed land increased every year. In many parts of England, the open-field system of crop farming was practised. However, some medieval landowners and farmers were changing to more modern ways of farming. Windmills were introduced in the late 12th century to drain the flatter lands of eastern Britain. Ploughing with horses instead of oxen allowed farmers to plough faster and over larger fields. After the Black Death there were fewer serfs to work as farm labourers, so landowners switched to the less labour intensive farming of sheep and cattle.

Medieval farmers gathering in the hay. Although this looks like an ancient scene, farming methods changed a great deal during the Middle Ages.

A Cash Economy

In the early Middle Ages, a tenant usually paid his rent by acting as a soldier for his lord. By 1150, many tenants paid a cash rent instead. Many lords preferred money payments so that they could hire professional troops. Royal mints issued ever larger amounts of currency and more services could be bought for cash in the towns.

Medieval Women

Most medieval women were peasant farmers who suffered hard lives full of backbreaking work raising crops and families. Some worked as servants in the households of rich merchants or noblemen. Only a few wealthy women were educated and enjoyed a more privileged life.

These medieval ladies of leisure wear gowns with deep 'V' necklines, narrow sleeves and fur cuffs. Their conical headdresses with veils are also typical of the time.

Women at Work

Nine out of ten women in medieval Britain lived and worked on farms, where they often had to do the same jobs as men. A list of wages on a farm estate in 1260 tells us that women were only paid about half as much as men for the same work. In the towns, only boys were allowed to join the trade guilds that trained craftsmen for the skilled, better paid jobs. Most townswomen were simply expected to marry, raise a family and run their husband's household.

Bond Servants

Perhaps the saddest women in medieval Britain were the bond servants, who were treated as slaves by their masters. A 13th-century document tells us something about their lives: 'A bond servant woman is put to hard work, toiling and slubbering [cleaning]. A bond servant woman is bought and sold like a beast and is not permitted to take a husband of her own choosing. She suffers many wrongs and is beaten with rods.'

Medieval Marriage

In the Middle Ages, few girls were able to choose their husband. Most could only marry with their parents' consent and many had to marry a man chosen by their father. Divorce was impossible for all except the very richest women, who could sometimes pay the Church to have their marriage annulled (cancelled). Girls from wealthy noble families were often married at the early age of twelve, usually to much older men. These young brides were expected to produce sons and often spent much of their married life pregnant. Many died in childbirth or soon after, for there were few doctors, and hygiene in most medieval houses was very poor.

Famous Women

The medieval women we know most about are those who acted in a manly way by ruling like kings or leading their armies in time of war. Catherine Douglas, the Countess of Dunbar, wore armour and fought on the battlements alongside her men when her castle was besieged in 1337. Queen Margaret of Anjou was married to England's Henry VI. He was weak and a poor leader, so Margaret led his troops against his enemies in the Wars of the Roses in the 1460s and 1470s. One of the richest medieval women was Devorguilla Balliol, who owned large estates in Scotland, England and France. She is remembered because she left much of her fortune to build a college in Oxford in 1282.

Medieval woman of action: the courageous Kate Barlass used her arm as a door bolt in an attempt to protect James I from murderous assassins in 1437.

Changing Life in Late Medieval Britain

The wars of the later Middle Ages made people feel more patriotic. The wars also added to the powers of the English Parliament.

Magna Carta was a document setting out the powers of the king and Parliament. This is the third version, issued in 1225.

Kings of One Nation

In the 12th century, the kings of Scotland and England could have exchanged their thrones and been happily accepted as king by their new subjects. By the 14th century however, people in many parts of Europe, including Britain, began to feel that they belonged to a particular nation. The Welsh and Scottish became much more patriotic during their struggles against English invasion. The English also felt more patriotic as a result of their long wars with France. The Hundred Years' War started as a fight between two kings, but ended as a struggle between two nations.

Writers and Languages

After 1350, more people were learning how to read and write. This changed the way that people thought about themselves. Scottish authors wrote down the heroic stories of Wallace and Bruce. Welsh poets kept alive the history and legends of their people. In England, Latin and French died out as languages of everyday use as men and women of all classes used English instead. Popular stories such as Geoffrey Chaucer's *The Canterbury Tales* were important in making the English feel more confident.

28

Kings and Freedoms

By 1350 the English Parliament had slowly begun to change from being the king's council of nobles into a national body that represented the people. In charters such as Magna Carta, kings were sometimes forced to admit that there were limits to their powers. They were also often bankrupted by long wars and forced to ask their people, through Parliament, for money. The English Parliament slowly built up its freedom by winning privileges, such as the 1362 right to decide how much tax should be paid on woollen goods. In the 1320 Declaration of Arbroath, the community or people of Scotland even stated that the king had to have 'the due consent and assent of us all' and that the people could get rid of a king who broke the laws of the kingdom. Parliament was slowly becoming more important, even if a powerful king could still do much as he pleased.

This artist's interpretation of Chaucer's The Canterbury Tales *shows the pilgrims gathering together at the Tabard Inn in Southwark, London, before their journey to Kent.*

The End of the Middle Ages

Throughout the Middle Ages, the landscape of Britain was dominated by stone castles where lords and knights controlled their lands. Behind their thick walls, lords could even defy the king. By 1450 this situation was changing, thanks to the coming of artillery guns that could blast holes in castle defences. This was one sign, among many, that the world of the Middle Ages was passing and that the countries of Britain were entering a new age.

Timeline

1215	• Magna Carta sets limits on the power of King John
1320	• Declaration of Arbroath
1337-1453	• Hundred Years' War deepens feelings of English patriotism
1375	• John Barbour, the Scottish poet, writes the epic poem *The Brus*
1380-90s	• Geoffrey Chaucer writes *The Canterbury Tales*
1450	• Siege guns become more effective against stone castles

Glossary

abdicate to give up the throne

artillery large guns made after 1400, usually used to attack castles

bankrupt to have spent all your money and have no more income

birlinn fast boat or galley used by the people of western Scotland

borough a town or area with some powers of self-government

burgh Scottish word for 'borough' (see above)

cavalry soldiers on horseback

cesspool underground pit where toilet waste was stored in medieval towns

charter a medieval document that usually recorded a person's property and privileges

chronicler someone, like a historian, who recorded events in medieval times

crusades military campaigns carried out by Christians in the Middle Ages to recapture the Holy Land from Muslims

dysentery a violent, exhausting disease caused by poor toilet hygiene

empire a collection of different countries ruled by one person

feudalism a medieval social system in which lords had control of the land and employed peasants to work it and serve the lords in times of war

Flemish people from Flanders in modern-day Belgium

Gaels a Celtic people

Galwegians people from Galloway in south-west Scotland

guerrilla a soldier who ambushes the enemy instead of fighting him in large battles

harrying attacking repeatedly

independent to be free and have no higher master or king

keep a high stone tower at the heart of a medieval castle

Latin the language of ancient Rome and the medieval Roman Catholic Church

mercenary a soldier who fights for pay rather than for his country or beliefs

Middle Ages the period of history between around 1000 and 1400 CE

mint to make coins, also the government office that makes coins

mutilate to cut a body savagely into pieces

Norn the medieval Norse language of parts of northern Scotland

Norse people from Norway or Scandinavia

patriot someone who feels deeply for his/her country

Plantagenet a line of English kings, ruling from 1154 (when Henry II came to the throne) to 1485 (the death of Richard III)

privilege the right or freedom to do something

regalia the crown, sceptre and jewels used in a coronation ceremony

sheriff a representative of royal authority in a shire, or area

stockade a defensive barrier of wooden posts driven upright side by side into the ground

tenant someone who rents land or property, usually to farm it

trade guild an organization made up of tradesmen and existing to protect their business interests

urban a word describing anything to do with towns and cities

Vikings Scandinavian people who raided the coasts of northern and western Europe from the 8th to the 10th centuries

Timeline

1066	• Norman invasion of England
1070	• William the Conqueror enforces his grip on England
1086	• England's wealth recorded in the *Domesday Book*
1100-1200	• Church in Wales falls under English influence and control
1100-35	• Reign of Henry I ('Beauclerc') who lays down many of the ways that England is governed
1124-53	• Reign of David I, a 'Normanizing' King of Scots
1171	• Henry II of England takes the lordship of Ireland
1204	• English kings lose control of their Normandy homelands
1215	• King John grants privileges to the English nobles in Magna Carta
1280	• High point of English control of eastern Ireland
1280	• Edward I begins building stone castles across northern Wales
1282	• Death of Llywelyn, last independent Welsh prince
1297	• William Wallace defeats the English at Stirling Bridge
1314	• Robert the Bruce defeats Edward II at Bannockburn
1320	• Scots' Declaration of Arbroath proclaims their independence
1337-1453	• Hundred Years' War between England and France
1349-50	• Black Death ravages the British and Irish Isles
1380-90	• Geoffrey Chaucer writes *The Canterbury Tales*
1400	• High point of the Gaelic-speaking MacDonald lordship of the isles
1415	• English victory over the French at Agincourt
1460-83	• Wars of the Roses between the Houses of Lancaster and York

Further Information

Books

Medieval Britain, History from Buildings, Peter Hepplewhite, Franklin Watts, 2006

Look Around a Medieval Castle, Clare Hibbert, Franklin Watts, 2007

Cathedrals and the Church, Pat Levy, Franklin Watts, 2006

Scotland in the Middle Ages 400–1450, Richard Dargie, Pulse Publications, 2001

Websites

www.royal.gov.uk/output/Page1.asp
the official website of the British monarchy containing detailed biographies of all the kings and queens of medieval Scotland and England

http://normans.etrusia.co.uk/
simple, clearly illustrated website with features on all aspects of life in Norman times

http://www.britainexpress.com/History/medieval_britain_index.htm
clearly written, illustrated website with short articles on all aspects of life in medieval England, from the Norman Conquest to the Wars of the Roses

http://www.bbc.co.uk/history/british/
detailed and well-illustrated web sections on the Normans and Britain in the Middle Ages with text articles, timelines, interactive games and links to relevant museum material

http://www.ltscotland.org.uk/scottishhistory/middleages/index.asp
a range of accessible resources on life in medieval Scotland with a focus upon the Wars of Scottish Independence

http://www.castlewales.com/medwales.html
well-constructed and comprehensive website on medieval Wales, with many interesting links; written in adult but accessible language

Index